Hip-hop USA

Hip-hop Culture

Wendy Garofoli

Consultant:
Emmett G. Price III, PhD
Chair, Department of African American Studies
Associate Professor of Music and African American Studies
Northeastern University
Boston, Massachusetts, USA

www.raintreepublishers.co.uk
Visit our website to find out
more information about
Raintree books.

To order:
☎ Phone 0845 6044371
📄 Fax +44 (0) 1865 312263
📧 Email myorders@raintreepublishers.co.uk

Customers from outside the UK please telephone +44 1865 312262

Raintree is an imprint of Capstone Global Library Limited, a company incorporated in England and Wales having its registered office at 7 Pilgrim Street, London, EC4V 6LB – Registered company number: 6695582

Text © Capstone Press 2011
First published in the United Kingdom in hardback by Capstone Global Library Ltd in 2011
The moral rights of the proprietor have been asserted.

Edited by Diyan Leake
Designed by Ashlee Suker
Originated by Capstone Global Library Ltd
Printed in and bound in China by Leo Paper Products Ltd

ISBN 978 1 406 21823 7 (hardback)
14 13 12 11 10
10 9 8 7 6 5 4 3 2 1

British Library Cataloguing in Publication Data
Garofoli, Wendy
Hip-hop culture. – (Hip-hop USA)
A full catalogue record for this book is available from the British Library.

Acknowledgements
We would like to thank the following for permission to reproduce photographs: Alamy/Everynight Images, cover; Alamy/Michael Shuttleworth, 45; Alamy/William S. Kuta, 16 (bottom); Alexander Yakovlev/123RF, 32; Capstone Studio/Karon Dubke, 34 (both), 40 (top), 41 (both), 43 (both); Corbis/Laura Levine, 17; David Lachapelle Studios/HSI/Darkfibre Ent/The Kobal Collection, 33; Getty Images Inc./Al Pereira/Michael Oachs Archives, 8; Getty Images Inc./China Photos, 30; Getty Images Inc./Chris Polk/FilmMagic, 35; Getty Images Inc./David Corio/Michael Oachs Archives, 39; Getty Images Inc./David Corio/Redferns, 19; Getty Images Inc./F. Roy Kemp/BIPs, 14; Getty Images Inc./George Karger/Pix Inc./Time & Life Pictures, 7; Getty Images Inc./Kerstin Rodgers/Redferns, 26; Getty Images Inc./Michael Ochs Archives, 37; Getty Images Inc./Santi Visalli, 9; iStockphoto/seraficus, 13 (top); Landov LLC/Bonnie Weller/MCT, 10; Landov LLC/Rose Prouser/Reuters, 40 (bottom); Newscom, 23 (bottom); Newscom/FayesVision/WENN, 42; Shutterstock/Andrei Nekrassov, 27 (bottom); Shutterstock/bg_knight, 44; Shutterstock/Corepics, 24; Shutterstock/Diane Garcia, 6; Shutterstock/djgis, 12 (top); Shutterstock/Edyta Pawlowska, 31; Shutterstock/emin kuliyer, 11; Shutterstock/Evgeny Litvinov, 22–23; Shutterstock/Franck Boston, 16 (spray can); Shutterstock/fritzkocher, 36; Shutterstock/John A. Anderson, 12 (bottom); Shutterstock/Joseph McCullar, 20 (top right); Shutterstock/kentoh, 42 (grunge background); Shutterstock/krupinina, 24 (black graffiti); Shutterstock/Kulish Viktoria, 20 (top left); Shutterstock/Lev Oikha, 29; Shutterstock/Myotis, 16 (sketchbook); Shutterstock/pandapaw, 18; Shutterstock/Peter Hestbaek, 21 (bottom); Shutterstock/pjcross, 13 (bottom); Shutterstock/Ramzi Hachicho, 15; Shutterstock/Sergei Bachlakov, 4–5; Shutterstock/Sergey Sklezney, 20 (bottom); Shutterstock/spaxiax, 21 (top); Shutterstock/tobe_dw, 27 (top); Shutterstock/Tomasz Trojanowski, 28; Shutterstock/VectorZilla, 16 (graffiti marker tag); www.dmcworld.com, 25.

Every effort has been made to contact copyright holders of material reproduced in this book. Any omissions will be rectified in subsequent printings if notice is given to the publisher.

CONTENTS

The roots

Flashy dance moves. Swift-fingered DJs. Daring graffiti artists. Hip-hop **culture** is made up of all these elements and more. It's a movement that began before hip-hop had a name.

Hip-hop's pioneers started with four pillars of expression — graffiti, DJ-ing, breakdancing, and MC-ing. These are the building blocks of hip-hop. Today, this American culture has spread around the world.

culture	set of social practices associated with a particular activity

4

THE FOUR ELEMENTS OF HIP-HOP

Hip-hop's pioneers used existing styles of music, art, and dance to create a whole new culture.

GRAFFITI: letters or pictures painted, scratched, or marked onto a piece of public property

DJ-ING: playing pre-recorded music for a radio, party, or club audience. *DJ* is short for *disc jockey*.

BREAKDANCING: a form of street dance that features footwork, floor work, and other acrobatic moves

MC-ING: rapping and rhyming over the beats of a DJ or producer. *MC* is short for *master of ceremonies*.

5

ORIGINS OF tHE FOUR ELEMENtS

The four basic elements of hip-hop culture did not spring out of thin air. They each grew from activities practised long before hip-hop began.

» Graffiti can be traced back to early rock drawings.

Atlantic Ocean

Jamaica

» DJs have been around since the first radio broadcast in the early 1900s. But hip-hop's DJ roots come from Jamaica. Beginning in the 1950s, Jamaican DJs played records over loud sound systems at street parties.

Swing dancing

Brazil

South America

>> Breakdancers get their moves
from elements of swing dancing
and a Brazilian dance style called
capoeira.

>> MCs get their rhymes from spoken-word poets,
African storytellers, and jazz singers who "scat sing".
They use short syllables such as "be-bop" to create
rhythmic sounds.

capoeira	a Brazilian dance of African origin that uses martial arts moves such as kicks and chops
rhythmic	having a regular beat in music or dance

IF It WEREN't FOR tHE BRONX

In the 1970s, the Bronx in New York City was a tough place to live. Crime, illegal drug use, and violence were on the rise. Many families were poor. Yet hip-hop culture grew out of this landscape.

The Bronx, 1972

AFRIKA BAMBAATAA

Afrika Bambaataa was originally the leader of a Bronx **gang** called the Black Spades. He gave up gang life in the early 1970s to become a DJ. Bambaataa formed the Zulu Nation, a group that helped spread positive hip-hop culture. Today, the Zulu Nation has members across the globe.

Early hip-hoppers invented positive ways to deal with hardship. Graffiti started as a way for gang members to mark their territory. But it became a type of artistic expression. DJs threw street parties where people could gather peacefully and dance. Breakdancers, also called b-boys and b-girls, competed at these parties. MCs pumped up the crowd with simple phrases such as "Clap ya hands".

gang organized group of people whose members are very loyal to one another. Some gang members take part in violent or illegal behaviour.

CHAPTER 1

Graffiti

Hip-hop graffiti started in Philadelphia in the 1960s. Darryl "Cornbread" McCray scribbled "Cornbread loves Cynthia" on the walls of his school. He then wrote "Cornbread" all over the city. Cornbread is considered the godfather of hip-hop graffiti.

Cornbread once wrote graffiti on an elephant at the Philadelphia Zoo.

Cornbread

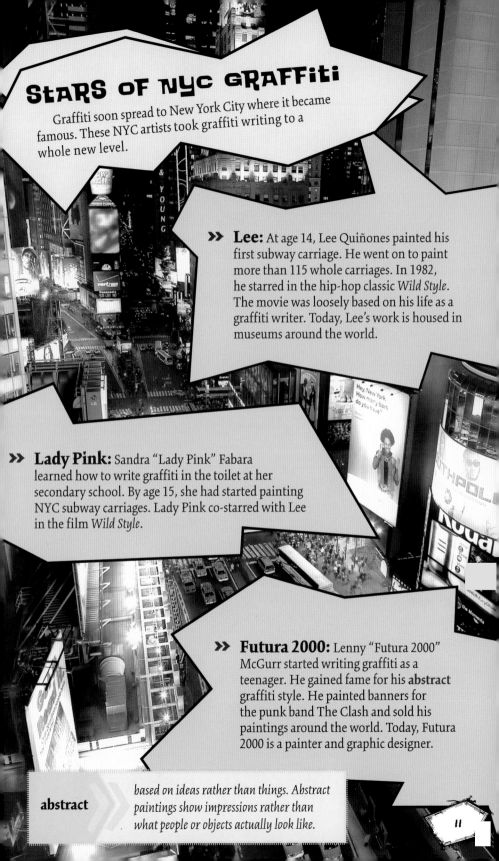

StaRS OF nYC GRAFFiti

Graffiti soon spread to New York City where it became famous. These NYC artists took graffiti writing to a whole new level.

» Lee: At age 14, Lee Quiñones painted his first subway carriage. He went on to paint more than 115 whole carriages. In 1982, he starred in the hip-hop classic *Wild Style*. The movie was loosely based on his life as a graffiti writer. Today, Lee's work is housed in museums around the world.

» Lady Pink: Sandra "Lady Pink" Fabara learned how to write graffiti in the toilet at her secondary school. By age 15, she had started painting NYC subway carriages. Lady Pink co-starred with Lee in the film *Wild Style*.

» Futura 2000: Lenny "Futura 2000" McGurr started writing graffiti as a teenager. He gained fame for his **abstract** graffiti style. He painted banners for the punk band The Clash and sold his paintings around the world. Today, Futura 2000 is a painter and graphic designer.

abstract	»»	based on ideas rather than things. Abstract paintings show impressions rather than what people or objects actually look like.

TYPES OF GRAFFITI

Each hip-hop graffiti artist has his or her own style. The best styles become blueprints for future artists. Here are some common forms of graffiti:

» **tag:** name written in signature lettering using permanent marker or spray paint

» **throw-up or fill-in:** quick outline of letters on a coloured background

12

>> **blockbuster:** evenly spaced, large square letters that are easy to read

>> **wild style:** complex form of graffiti using interlocking arrows, letters, and connecting points

The word *graffiti* is from the Italian word *graffiare*, which means "to scratch".

GRAFFiTi iN NYC: A TiMELiNE

Graffiti may have started in Philadelphia, but it took off in the Big Apple. Take a look at New York City graffiti history:

1968: Julio 204 tags his name and street number using permanent marker and spray paint.

1973: Graffiti covers entire subway lines and buses.

1972: Super Kool 223 is believed to write the first multi-coloured work, called a "piece". Super Kool also creates the first "top to bottom" when he draws on the entire side of a subway carriage.

Mid-1970s: Tracy 168 creates wild style.

1972: Mayor John Lindsay declares war on graffiti.

1971: The *New York Times* prints a story about a young boy named Demetrius who writes graffiti. He lives on 183rd Street and tags "Taki 183". Within a year of the article, hundreds of others start writing graffiti.

1980: Blade and Comet I create blockbuster style. They each paint more than 5,000 trains.

1977: Writers such as Lee, Futura 2000, and Lady Pink become known as graffiti stars.

1986: With increased subway security, only diehard graffiti artists, such as Ghost, Sento, and Sane, continue to tag the cars.

Late 1970s: The Transit Authority creates a giant subway carriage wash. This stops some graffiti artists from painting the carriages again.

1982: The city starts to gain the upper hand against graffiti writers. Young people can't buy spray paint as easily. The subway depots are more closely guarded.

1989: The last fully graffitied subway car is removed from service.

1981: Some graffiti artists become fed up when newcomers paint over their work. They begin putting their pieces on canvas instead of public property.

GLOBAL GRAFFITI

Although graffiti began as an American practice, it is now popular worldwide. Graffiti's influence spread when artists Henry Chalfant and Martha Cooper published the book *Subway Art* in 1984. Filmmakers also had a hand in spreading graffiti culture. In the early 1980s, hip-hop films *Style Wars* and *Wild Style* featured graffiti art. By the end of the decade, many Europeans were hooked. Some Europeans even made the journey to New York City to tag the birthplace of hip-hop.

A PLANNED PIECE

In the 1970s and 1980s, many graffiti writers planned out their pieces before heading to the train depots. They bought sketchbooks filled with plain white paper. Then they drew their pieces using markers and coloured pencils.

Graffiti was popular during World War II (1939–1945). US soldiers would write the phrase "Kilroy was here" next to a drawing wherever they went. Legend has it that shipyard inspector James J. Kilroy started the craze. He wrote "Kilroy was here" to show he had inspected a ship.

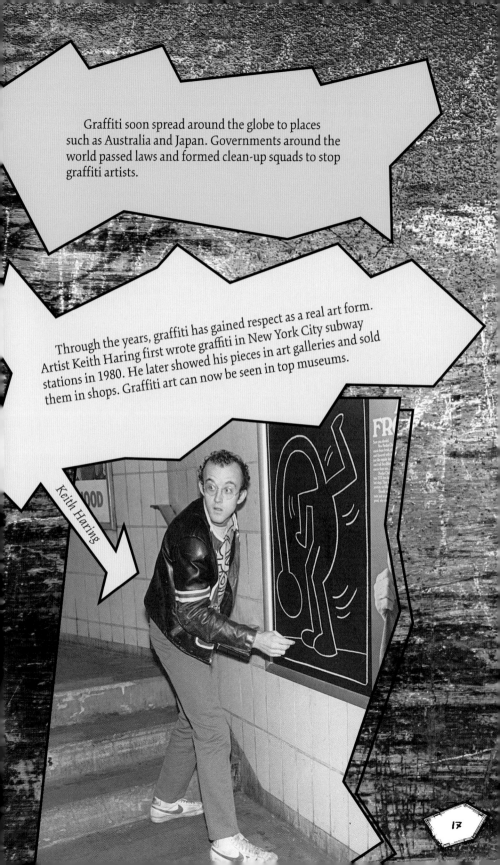

Graffiti soon spread around the globe to places such as Australia and Japan. Governments around the world passed laws and formed clean-up squads to stop graffiti artists.

Through the years, graffiti has gained respect as a real art form. Artist Keith Haring first wrote graffiti in New York City subway stations in 1980. He later showed his pieces in art galleries and sold them in shops. Graffiti art can now be seen in top museums.

Keith Haring

CHAPTER 2

DJ-ing

DJ Kool Herc was hip-hop's first star. He is known as the father of hip-hop. Herc came to the United States from Jamaica in 1967. He began DJ-ing in the Bronx in New York City in 1973. Instead of playing the whole song, Herc set his records to the drum break. He would buy two copies of the same record. Then he switched back and forth between them to feature the break section. This section became known as the "break beat".

platter – *plate on which the record sits. The platter spins the record.*

needle – *metal piece that sits in the record's grooves. Waves in the grooves cause vibrations, which become electrical signals played by the speakers.*

Two other Bronx DJs played key roles in the early hip-hop movement. Afrika Bambaataa left gang life behind to play at street parties in the Bronx. Bambaataa spun little-known records, which earned him the nickname "Master of Records".

In the mid-1970s, Grandmaster Flash brought DJ-ing to another level. He had unmatched technical skills and hand-eye coordination. Flash and his crew developed a wide range of DJ techniques still used today. They invented **cutting**, the **needle drop**, and the **scratch**. They also introduced the beat box, a drum machine played in time with the song.

Grandmaster Flash

cutting	seamlessly switching from one record to the next
needle drop	action of dropping the needle on a specific spot on the record
scratch	action of moving a record back and forth while the needle is dropped

How to DJ

DJ-ing is a craft that calls for special equipment to pull it off. Some basic equipment used by DJs includes:

>> sound recordings: pre-recorded music, such as records, CDs, or MP3 files

>> turntables: combination of two record players. DJs switch back and forth between turntables in order to create endless sound.

>> headphones: pair of earphones joined by a headband. DJs use headphones to listen to one recording while the other is played to the audience.

mixer: device that fades out one song as another fades in. A mixer allows a DJ to move smoothly between songs.

slipmat: mat that is placed between the record and the turntable platter. A slipmat allows the DJ to hold the record still while the platter spins beneath it.

sound system: speakers and amplifiers broadcast the sound

Once a DJ has the necessary equipment, it's time to master a few basic skills.

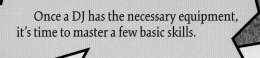

>> **scratching:** moving the record back and forth under the needle in a rhythmic way

>> **beat matching:** matching the tempo of one song to the next. DJs change the **pitch** or speed of one song until it matches the beat of the other song; this allows a DJ to switch smoothly from one song to the next.

>> **cutting:** switching from one record to the next; once both records are beat matched, the DJ will quickly cut or fade over to the other record.

pitch >> *the highness or lowness of a sound*

beat juggling: playing two drum patterns on two different turntables. DJs juggle back and forth to create a new beat.

backspinning: spinning a record backwards while the platter below it spins forwards. Backspinning is often used when cutting or beat juggling.

DJ SCRATCH

DJ Scratch is a top hip-hop DJ and producer. He gained fame in the late 1980s while touring with rap group Run-DMC. He has since produced songs for 50 Cent, LL Cool J, and Busta Rhymes. He has also DJ'd for rap superstars Diddy and Jay-Z at their concerts.

THE DiGiTAL DJ

When hip-hop DJ-ing began, DJs filled boxes with records and lugged them to their shows. Today, most DJs play MP3s off their computers or iPods. With thousands of song options at their fingertips, they quickly choose songs to match the crowd's mood. DJs use music storage programs such as iTunes to organize their music. They can mix songs together on the computer and burn them to a disc. CD scratch machines even allow DJs to scratch the discs, much like they would records. Software programs, such as Pitch 'N Time and Scratch Live, let DJs mix and scratch digital files.

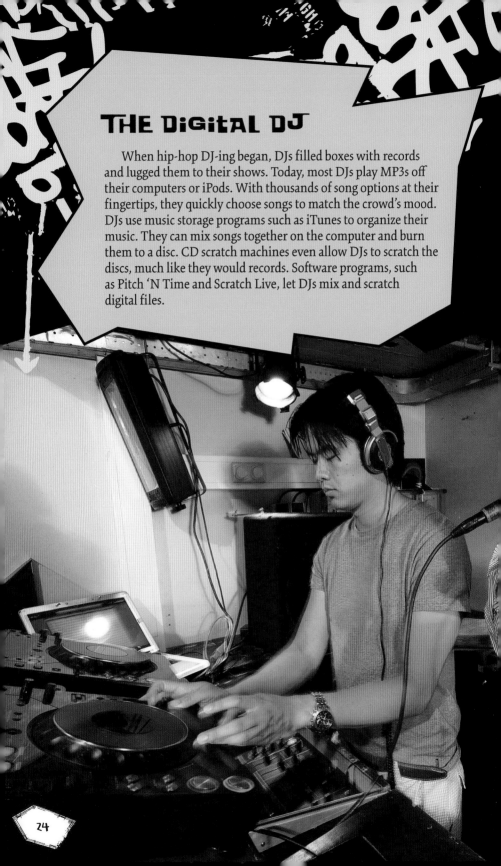

TURNTABLISM

Turntablism is the act of playing the turntable as a musical instrument. During the 1980s and 1990s, machines replaced the DJ in the recording studio and on stage. DJs had to find new ways to perform. They invented new styles of scratching, backspinning, and beat juggling to create their own sounds. The style changed into a physical performance. DJs spun records behind their backs, with their elbows, and even while removing their shirts.

Today, turntablists fight it out in international battles. One such battle is the DMC World DJ Championship held each year in London. DJs from more than 25 countries compete to see who is the best in the world.

CHAPTER 3

Breakdancing

The Bronx was the birthplace of another hip-hop pillar – breakdancing. Breakdancing is often called breaking or b-boying. Early dancers performed to the drum beat section of a record, called the break beat. These b-boys and b-girls showed off their moves at the parties of DJs Kool Herc and Afrika Bambaataa.

As hip-hop moved from the underground to the mainstream, so did breakdancing. What was once performed at parties or on the street appeared in adverts, TV shows, and films. By the mid-1980s, breakdancing had become a worldwide craze.

Legendary NYC breakdancing crews the Dynamic Rockers and Rock Steady Crew battled one another in the 1983 film *Style Wars*.

While breakdancing's popularity soared, some felt the style was becoming overexposed. Many of hip-hop's DJs and MCs who had supported breakdancing turned their backs on it. Members of the media, which had once celebrated the dance, called b-boying a fad. By the end of the 1980s, breakdancing had disappeared from the spotlight. But diehard fans kept it alive.

BREAKDANCING GEAR

There's no set uniform for breakdancing. But many b-boys and b-girls come prepared with items that are comfortable, safe, and expressive. Typical breaker gear includes:

» baggy trousers and T-shirts for ease of movement

» wrist and elbow bands for cushioning during arm freezes

» trainers to keep the feet from slipping

» helmet, bandana, or beanie cap to protect head while headspinning

BREAKING TERMS AND MOVES

Breakdancers use their own vocabulary to describe what they do. Here are some common breakdancing terms and moves:

» **top rocking:** footwork performed while standing up; breakdancers rock their bodies back and forth to warm up and feel the beat before they head to the floor.

» **six-step:** a floor move performed in six steps; breakdancers place their palms on the ground and rotate their feet and body in a circle.

» **battle:** competition between individual dancers or groups. The dancers who receive the loudest crowd applause win.

» **crew:** group of dancers that rehearses and performs together

» **freeze:** pause in the middle of a move to add drama

29

» **k-kick:** one-handed handstand in which the body forms the shape of a "K"

» **windmill:** a spinning move. Breakdancers roll their torsos on the ground while whipping their legs around in a "V" shape.

The Rock Steady Crew invented many breaking moves, including the windmill and a spinning handstand called the 1990.

headspin: a spinning move performed on one's head

hollowback: handstand with an arched back

Funk Styles

Breakdancing isn't the only type of hip-hop dance. Many styles came out of the West Coast of the United States during the late 1960s and early 1970s. These dances are called the funk styles. In the late 1960s, Don Campbell invented locking when he had trouble doing the funky chicken dance. Locking is made up of bold, playful movements.

Boogaloo Sam of the dance group the Electric Boogaloos invented popping in the mid-1970s. This style includes sharp ticks of the muscles, resulting in a robotic look.

Floating is another popular funk style. Dancers appear to float across the floor by sliding their feet.

locking

Michael Jackson made floating famous when he performed the backslide at the 1983 Motown 25th Anniversary Special. He called this move the moonwalk.

krumping

KRUMPING

Krumping is a wild, body-shaking style of hip-hop dance. Thomas "Tommy the Clown" Johnson invented krumping in the early 1990s. He performed as a clown at birthday parties in Los Angeles. Guests loved his playful "clown dancing". Johnson soon taught others how to krump. In 2008, he teamed up with rapper Snoop Dogg to set up krumping battles for young people. Kids can compete to see who has the best moves.

BREAKDANCING COMES FULL CIRCLE

Breakdancing is more popular today than it was in the 1980s. The style has been featured in movies such as *You Got Served* and *Step Up 2: The Streets*. Hip-hop dance crews such as the Groovaloos from Los Angeles breakdance all over the United States. Battles happen on a global scale, with competitions taking place from Canada to Germany. Hip-hop dance, from breaking to newer styles such as krumping, remains an important part of hip-hop culture.

WIDESCREEN

Step Up

Two dancers.
Two worlds.
One dream.

DANCE-OFF EDITI

STEP UP 2
THE STREETS

Includes The #1
Smash Hit Music Video
"LOW"
By Flo Rida f/ T-Pain
Plus More Videos From

Missy Elliott
Cherish f/ Yung Joc
Plies f/ Akon
Brit & Alex

Quest Crew

AMERICA'S BEST DANCE CREW

In 2008, *American Idol* judge Randy Jackson and MTV created a reality TV programme called *America's Best Dance Crew (ABDC)*. The programme's producers hold auditions across the United States to find the best dance groups. Crews often perform hip-hop moves such as breakdancing and popping. The top crews throw down their best moves. Winners receive a $100,000 prize.

ABDC WINNERS

Season 1
JabbaWockeeZ

Season 2
Super Cr3w

Season 3
Quest Crew

Season 4
We Are Heroes

MC-ing

MC-ing is the best-known part of hip-hop culture. MCs are basically today's rappers. But MCs didn't start off as the big stars they are today. DJs first hired MCs to help pump up the crowd. At Kool Herc and Afrika Bambaataa's parties, MCs called out simple phrases such as "Say, Oh Yeah!"

MCs brought their performances to another level at DJ Grandmaster Flash's parties. Flash had five MCs, called the Furious Five. They rhymed back and forth and created dance moves. The Furious Five switched the spotlight from the DJ to the MC.

In 1979, MCs made the jump from party favourites to hit makers. The single "Rapper's Delight" by the Sugarhill Gang peaked at number four on the *Billboard* R&B chart. "Rapper's Delight" was the world's introduction to hip-hop music. More than 30 years later, MCs continue to rule popular music and culture.

Sugarhill Gang

The Sugarhill Gang was the first act signed to the hip-hop label Sugar Hill Records.

HiP-HoP SNaP SHotS

From hip-hop's birth, the best MCs had their own unique style and sound. Here's a look at MC trends through the years:

>> **Early 1980s: Old School**

The MCs — Kurtis Blow, Run-DMC, LL Cool J

The Sound — funky, storytelling rhymes

The Look — track suits, Adidas trainers, fedoras or Kangol hats

BEATBOXING

Beatboxing is a kind of vocal percussion that is popular in hip-hop music. Beatboxers use their lips, tongue, throat, and voice to create sounds and beats. In the 1980s, beatboxing made its first public appearances. In 1983, a group called the Fat Boys won a New York City talent contest by beatboxing. Rapper Doug E. Fresh showcased his beatboxing skills in the 1984 movie *Beat Street*. In the mid-1980s, Biz Markie took beatboxing to another level by rapping in between his self-made beats.

Beatboxing faded from popularity in the 1990s. But in the 2000s, artists such as Justin Timberlake picked up the style. Today, beatbox conventions and battles are held around the world.

Biz Markie teaches kids how to beatbox on a US programme called *Yo Gabba Gabba!*

▸▸ Mid- to late 1980s: Rock and Rap

The MCs — Ice-T, Public Enemy, Eric B. and Rakim

The Sound — tough, truth-telling lyrics

The Look — bandanas, black leather jackets, giant gold chains

Eric B. and Rakim

▸▸ Early 1990s: Commercial Rap

The MCs — MC Hammer, Salt-N-Pepa, Kris Kross, Sir Mix-a-Lot

The Sound — party music; fast, playful lyrics and beats

The Look — Hammer pants, bold neon colours, baggy clothes

2PAC
ME
AGAINST
THE
WORLD

» Mid-1990s: Gangsta Rap

The MCs — Dr. Dre, Tupac Shakur, the Notorious B.I.G.

The Sound — hard lyrics about gangs and street life; chilled-out beats

The Look — Converse trainers, baseball caps, flannel T-shirts, sweatshirts

» Late 1990s: Bling-Bling

The MCs — Mase, Diddy, Jay-Z, Lil' Kim, Foxy Brown

The Sound — sampled 1980s tracks with boastful rhymes about money, cars, and fashion labels

The Look — slick suits, diamond bling, high-end fashion labels

Lil' Kim

sample ▷▷ *to take a portion of one song and reuse it in another*

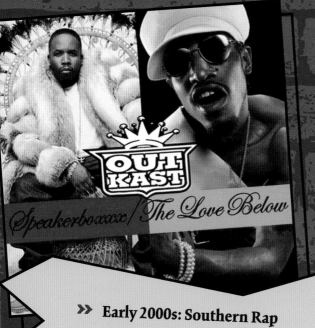

Speakerboxxx / The Love Below

>> **Early 2000s: Southern Rap**

The MCs — Lil Jon, Ludacris, OutKast, Lil Wayne

The Sound — gritty Southern crunk, a rap style with catchy refrains and a heavy beat

The Look — fatigue trousers, hoodies, grillz, message T-shirts

Kanye West's Graduation album

>> **Mid-to-Late 2000s: Futuristic**

The MCs — T-Pain, T.I., Kanye West

The Sound — distorted vocals, stripped-down sound

The Look — anything goes!

WOMEN IN RAP

Female MCs have been a part of the hip-hop scene from the very beginning. Lady B recorded the first rap single by a female, "To the Beat Y'all", in 1980. Salt-N-Pepa, Queen Latifah, and MC Lyte gained commercial success at the end of the decade. These female rappers spoke about equality. MC Lyte became the first solo female rapper to have a record certified as gold in 1993 with her single "Ruffneck". The blunt, bold female rappers Lil' Kim, Foxy Brown, and Lauryn Hill ended the 1990s on a powerful note for women in hip-hop.

In the 2000s, Missy Elliott wowed fans with space-age beats and groundbreaking music videos. She proved that women could not only rule the charts but also become highly successful producers.

MC Lyte

The Recording Industry Association of America certifies a record as gold when it sells 500,000 copies.

TIME FOR FEMALE MCS

1980 – Lady B releases the first female rap single, "To the Beat Y'all".

1989 – At age 19, Queen Latifah releases *All Hail the Queen*. She is praised for her positive lyrics.

1993 – Salt-N-Pepa releases *Very Necessary*. The album sells more than 5 million copies.

1998 – Lauryn Hill wins five Grammy awards for her album *The Miseducation of Lauryn Hill*.

2009 – M.I.A. wins Best Female Hip-Hop Artist at the BET Awards.

MCS IN THE MOVIES

The life of the MC has popped up in several Hollywood films. In 2002, rapper Eminem starred in *8 Mile*. He played a struggling rapper. Rapper Ludacris lent his star power to 2005's *Hustle & Flow*. Both films took home the Academy Award for Best Original Song.

43

Global Hip-Hoppers

Imagine watching an MC grab the mic and start rapping – in Arabic. That's what fans were treated to at the Kennedy Center for the Performing Arts in Washington DC in the summer of 2009. Hip-hoppers from Argentina, Lebanon, Vietnam, the Philippines, and the Palestinian Territories travelled to the United States. They took to the stage to represent their home countries. They rapped and danced. Some added touches of the tango and salsa to their moves.

These artists took part in the US Department of State's Cultural Visitors Program. For three weeks, the group toured New York, Philadelphia, and Washington DC. They met US hip-hop artists and even rubbed shoulders with legends such as Afrika Bambaataa.

THE Beat goes on

Graffiti, DJ-ing, breakdancing, and MC-ing have been hip-hop's main creative outlets since the movement began. But hip-hop culture has also shaped fashion, language, politics, films, books, and much more. Hip-hop may have started in the Bronx, but its message has spread to every corner of the globe. Hip-hop culture is more than a trend. It's a way for people from all walks of life to connect.

A graffiti artist in England painted this mural in 2007.

GLOSSARY

abstract based on ideas rather than things. Abstract paintings show impressions rather than what people or objects actually look like.

bling flashy jewellery sometimes worn to show wealth

capoeira a Brazilian dance of African origin that uses martial arts moves such as kicks and chops

culture set of social practices associated with a particular activity

cut seamlessly switch from one record to the next

equality the same rights for everyone

gang an organized group of people whose members are very loyal to one another. Some gang members take part in violent or illegal behaviour.

media TV, radio, newspapers, and other communication forms that send out messages to large groups of people

needle drop action of dropping the needle on a specific spot on the record

pitch highness or lowness of a sound

rhythmic having a regular beat in music or dance

sample take a portion of one song and reuse it in another

scratch move a record back and forth while the needle is dropped

tag write one's name on public property in paint or permanent marker

FiND out MoRE

BOOKS

Cornish, Melanie J. *The History of Hip Hop*, Crabtree Contact
series (Crabtree, 2009).

Fitzgerald, Tamsin. *Hip-hop and Urban Dance*, Dance series
(Heinemann Library, 2008).

Hatch, Thomas. *A History of Hip-Hop: The Roots of Ra*, High
Five Reading series (Red Brick Learning, 2006).

Llanas, Sheila Griffin. *Hip-hop Stars*, Hip-hop USA series
(Raintree, 2011).

Waters, Rosa. *Hip-Hop: A Short History*, Hip-Hop series
(Mason Crest, 2007).

WEBSITES

www.ukbboy.info
   The UK's b-boy community website, containing news,
   moves, and info on competitions

www.britishhiphop.co.uk
   A website about British hiphop

www.commonsensemedia.org/music-review
   Go to the menu on the left of the page to find a list
   of hiphop music for kids

INDEX